MODEST PETROVICH MUSSORGSKY – MAURICE RAVEL

TABLEAUX D'UNE EXPOSITION
PICTURES AT AN EXHIBITION
BILDER EINER AUSSTELLUNG

for Orchestra

Edited by/Herausgegeben von
Arbie Orenstein

Ernst Eulenburg Ltd

London · Mainz · Madrid · New York · Paris · Prague · Tokyo · Toronto · Zürich

CONTENTS

PREFACE

Modest Mussorgsky (1839–1881) composed *Kartinki s vistavki* (*Pictures at an Exhibition*) in a burst of creative activity between 2 and 22 June 1874. The composer's title refers to a commemorative exhibition of paintings, water-colours and architectural designs by his col-league Victor Hartmann (1834–1873), that was organized in St Petersburg by their mutual friend Vladimir Stasov, the noted art critic. Mussorgsky described his new project in a letter to Stasov written in June 1874:

Hartmann is boiling as *Boris* [*Godunov*] boiled; sounds and ideas have been hanging in the air; I am devouring them and stuffing myself – I barely have time to scribble them on paper. I am writing the 4th number – the links are good (on 'promenade'). I want to finish it as quickly and securely as I can. My profile can be seen in the interludes. I consider it successful to this point.[1]

On 1 July Stasov wrote to Rimsky-Korsakov (1844–1908) about the second part of the piece:

[…] I feel that all the best things are there. 'The Gossipers of Limoges' at the market is a delightful Scherzino and is very pianistic. Then comes 'Baba-Yaga', which is magnificent and powerful, and, for the conclusion, 'The Bogatyrs' Gate at Kiev', in the manner of a hymn or finale à la 'Slavsia';[2] of course [it is] a hundred million times worse and weaker, but [it is] a beautiful, powerful, original piece just the same. There is a particularly beautiful church melody here, 'As You Are Baptized in Christ', and the sound of bells in an entirely new manner. In this same sec-ond part, there are some unusually poetic moments. These appear in the music for Hartmann's painting 'The Catacombs of Paris', which consists of nothing but skulls. At first Musoryanin has a depiction of a gloomy cavern (with purely orchestral chords held out long with a big ⌒). Then, above a tremolo in minor, comes the first promenade theme; this is the glimmering of little lights in the skulls; here, suddenly, Hartmann's enchanting, poetic appeal to Mussorgsky rings out […]. But don't imagine, admiral, that Musoryanin has only been applying himself to this [work]: now there suddenly has awakened in him such a desire for composition, that it seems hardly a day passes him by without it.[3]

Stasov's comments regarding the 'sound of bells' and 'purely orchestral chords' turned out to be prophetic: no other work for the piano has been orchestrated so often.

Mussorgsky's piano suite interprets 10 of Hartmann's works. In addition, five promenades are interspersed that capture the differing moods of the composer as he strolls from one picture to another. The promenades are all based on the opening promenade melody, which also appears in 'With the Dead in a Dead Language', and the finale, 'The Great Gate of Kiev', thus pro-ducing a broad cyclical unity. The pictures and their musical interpretations may be summa-rized as follows.

1. 'Gnomus' [Latin: The Gnome]. In a letter to a colleague, Stasov described this carved, wooden dwarf as 'a kind of nutcracker, a gnome into whose mouth you put a nut to crack'. The music, which is grotesque, nervous, and not with-out a touch of tragedy, is a spiritual ancestor of Ravel's 'Scarbo' from *Gaspard de la nuit.*

2. 'Il vecchio castello' [Italian: The Old Castle]. Hartmann's painting portrayed a me-dieval Italian castle, with a troubadour singing and accompanying himself on the lute. A pedal point on G sharp in the bass extends through-out the 107 bars of this hauntingly sustained serenade.

3. 'Tuileries (Dispute d'enfants après jeux)' [French: Tuileries (Children Quarrelling after Play)]. The artist's watercolour of this famous Parisian park highlighted a group of quarrelling children. Mussorgsky's playful interpretation

[1] Quoted in Alexandra Orlova, *Mussorgsky's Days and Works*, transl. and ed. Roy J. Guenther (Ann Arbor, 1983), 416

[2] Referring to the majestic finale for chorus and orchestra, 'Glory to the Tsar', from Glinka's opera *A life for the Tsar*

[3] Orlova, op. cit., 419–420

never exceeds *mezzo forte,* and his sensitivity to the pristine world of childhood is much in evidence. A similar melding of innocence and sophistication is found in Ravel's *Ma Mère l'Oye* and *L'Enfant et les sortilèges.*

4. 'Bydło' [Polish: Cattle]. Hartmann sketched a wagon with large wheels drawn by two oxen plodding along a muddy road. With its steady, lumbering rhythm and Slavic despondency, Mussorgsky's setting recalls Chopin's Prelude in A minor (Op. 28/2).

5. 'Balet nevylupivshikhsa ptentsov' [Russian: Ballet of the Unhatched Chicks]. This is the first of only three Russian titles in Mussorgsky's piece. Hartmann painted several watercolours for the costumes in a ballet by Julius Gerber entitled *Trilby,* which was staged in St Petersburg. Stasov explained that the scenario called for a group of little boys and girls dressed as canary-birds, who scampered on the stage. Mussorgsky's fleeting Lilliputian music is set in the form of a scherzo, trio, scherzo and coda.

6. 'Samuel Goldenberg und Schmuÿle' [German, perhaps Yiddish: Samuel Goldenberg and Schmuÿle]. The title would sound virtually the same in Yiddish, which Mussorgsky may have tried to convey by writing a diaeresis over the 'y'. The portraits were sketched in Sandomierz, Poland and Stasov later entitled them 'Two Jews: Rich and Poor'. Hartmann gave the portraits to Mussorgsky as a gesture of friendship, and the composer had them displayed at his colleague's exhibition. In a brief statement of his aesthetic views, Mussorgsky observed that:

Art is a means of communicating with people, not an end in itself [...]. The mission of the art of music [is] to be the reproduction in musical sounds of not only the nuances of the emotions, but, even more important, the nuances of human speech.[4]

The authoritative opening and the humiliating begging found in Mussorgsky's impressive dialogue admirably convey his aesthetic viewpoint.

7. 'Limoges. Le marché (La grande nouvelle)' [French: Limoges. The Market Place (Important News)]. Stasov asserted that Hartmann had painted a picture of a crowd in a market place in Limoges, France. The gossip, commotion, clatter and chatter in this piece (which reappear in Strauss's *Till Eulenspiegels lustige Streiche*) were interpreted in prose by Mussorgsky in his manuscript, but subsequently crossed out. He wrote in French:

Important news: Monsieur Pimpant de Panta-Pantaléon has just recovered his cow, 'Fugitive'. 'Yes, Ma'am, that was yesterday. No, Ma'am, it was the day before yesterday. Why yes, Ma'am, the beast roamed about the neighbourhood. Why no, Ma'am, the beast didn't roam at all.' Etc.

8. 'Catacombae (Sepulcrum romanum)' [Latin: Catacombs (A Roman Sepulchre)]. Hartmann's sombre watercolour portrayed himself, a colleague and a guide examining the catacombs in Paris. At the right are rows of human skulls. Mussorgsky's incorrect Latin title for the second part of this piece is written in pencil in his manuscript: 'Con [instead of "Cum"] Mortuis in Lingua Mortua' [With the Dead in a Dead Language].[5] He adds (in Russian): 'May well it be in Latin! The creative spirit of the late Hartmann leads me to the skulls and invokes them; gradually the skulls begin to glow.' The frightening gloom and touches of the supernatural found in this eerie diptych form a striking contrast with the carefree mood of the preceding piece.

9. 'Izbushka na kurynikh nozhkakh (Baba-Yaga)' [Russian: The Hut on Hen's Legs (Baba-Yaga)]. Hartmann's ornate pencil sketch showed a Russian-style clock as part of a witch's hut resting on hen's legs. A pounding, tempestuous opening section conjures up the wild flight of the witch Baba-Yaga, who eats human bones. The quieter middle section contains mysterious tremolos throughout, and a reprise of the opening section leads to a Lisztian coda which connects

---

[4] Malcolm Hamrick Brown, ed., *Mussorgsky in Memoriam 1881–1981* (Ann Arbor, 1982), 3

[5] Although correctly printed in Rimsky-Korsakov's first piano edition of *Pictures* ('Cum'), most subsequent editions (and Ravel's autograph) are incorrect ('Con').

this piece with the finale. Thus, after interpreting Hartmann's artistic excursions in Italy, France and Poland, the concluding pictures return to Russian folklore (Baba-Yaga) and Russian history (the finale).

10. 'Bogatyrskie vorota (vo stolnom gorode vo Kieve)' [Russian: The Knight's Gate (In the Ancient Capital City of Kiev)]. Hartmann's design for a ceremonial gateway was entered in a competition to commemorate an event which occurred in Kiev on 4 April 1866. The event, understandably suppressed by the censors, was an attempt to assassinate Tsar Alexander II, who escaped unharmed. (The competition was called off and the monument was never built.) Hartmann designed an arch resting on two pillars that contained a verse from Psalm 118: 'Blessed be he who comes in the name of the Lord.' Above the arch was a stained-glass chapel, a figure of the Archangel Michael and on top the Russian imperial eagle. To the right of the arch was a belfry. The composer's finale suggests a solemn processional, with massive chords, modal church chorales and bell-like sonorities, and concludes with a grandiose majesty that is strikingly orchestral.

It was the Russian-born American conductor Serge Koussevitzky (1874–1951) who commissioned Ravel to transcribe *Pictures at an Exhibition*. In a taped interview with this writer, Ravel's colleague and biographer Roland-Manuel recalled their musical activities during the summer of 1922.

I was privileged to watch Ravel orchestrating Mussorgsky's *Pictures at an Exhibition*. We were at my parents' home in the country [at Lyons-la-Fôret, some 60 miles northwest of Paris] where there was a room we shared which had a piano. We were seated side by side at the same table; I was orchestrating a song by Debussy, *Le Faune,* while Ravel was orchestrating Mussorgsky's *Pictures at an Exhibition* [...]. He would occasionally show me Mussorgsky's score and say: 'What instrument would you use here?' 'Perhaps,' I ventured on one occasion, 'a clarinet'. 'A clarinet?' he replied, 'that would intrude!' Very well, it would intrude. He thereupon returned to his work, and later said, 'Come look'. It wasn't a clarinet, it was a saxophone!

I saw – this was a great privilege – how he orchestrated. Of course it wasn't his own music, but it was nevertheless very interesting. He attentively examined the passage he was working on; he wrote, distributing the instruments like any other orchestrator. Then, very often, he went to the piano and isolated an instrumental group. He needed, he said, to hear what one group was doing in relation to the others. For example, he looked at what the strings were doing and played their parts on the piano. He said that he used the piano far more when orchestrating than when composing the first drafts of his own works.[6]

Regarding Ravel's need to isolate instrumental groups, it appears that many of his tuttis are organized by families of instruments, with each instrumental group (except of course the percussion) having the melody, harmony and the bass note (see the final bars of the opening 'Promenade' or the conclusion of 'The Great Gate of Kiev'). Ravel's ability to create unexpected, memorable orchestral sonorities is evident in his transcription: there are extended solos for the saxophone ('Il vecchio castello') and the tuba ('Bydło'); in 'Gnomus' (fig. 9) Mussorgsky repeats the preceding 10 bars but Ravel reorchestrates the passage, this time with the celesta (replacing the woodwinds) accompanied by string glissandos on the fingerboard; Schmuÿle's begging is conveyed (somewhat paradoxically!) by a muted trumpet playing *fortissimo* (fig. 58). In addition to many subtleties in the percussion section (for example at fig. 55 or from fig. 121ff.), one of Ravel's most striking passages for the brass family (accompanied by the woodwinds and double basses) appears in 'Catacombae'. In general, the transcription indicates a thorough assimilation of Rimsky-Korsakov's orchestral technique, coupled with Ravel's own penchant for a sound, as he put it, 'bathed in a sonorous fluid'.[7]

---

[6] This interview took place at the Paris apartment of Roland-Manuel on 1 February 1966.

[7] See Arbie Orenstein, *Ravel: Man and Musicians* (New York, 1991), 126. Ravel once remarked that there was always more to be learned in the art of orchestration. He not only orchestrated many of his own piano pieces, but also transcribed works by Chabrier, Chopin, Debussy, Schumann, Satie and others.

Although *Pictures at an Exhibition* is unquestionably Mussorgsky's most important composition for the piano, it was neglected by pianists for many years, both within Russia and abroad. Rather curiously, it was only after Ravel's transcription achieved worldwide recognition that pianists began to perform the piece. Professor Malcolm H. Brown has called Ravel's achievement 'a rare example of creative symbiosis whose artistic validity is granted by admirers of both composers',[8] and Arturo Toscanini stated that 'the two great treatises on instrumentation were the one written by Berlioz and Ravel's orchestration of *Pictures*'.[9]

In the last analysis, Ravel's transcription is a brilliant homage to Mussorgsky, whose music he had studied and deeply admired for many years.

Arbie Orenstein

[8] Brown, op. cit., 6
[9] Harvey Sachs, *Toscanini* (London, 1978), 316

VORWORT

Modest Mussorgskij (1839–1881) komponierte *Kartinki s vistavki (Bilder einer Ausstellung)* zwischen dem 2. und 22. Juni 1874 in einem wahren Schaffensrausch. Der Titel des Komponisten bezieht sich auf eine Gedenkausstellung mit Zeichnungen, Aquarellen und architektonischen Entwürfen seines Kollegen Viktor Hartmann (1834–1873), die von einem gemeinsamen Freund, dem bekannten Kunstkritiker Wladimir Stassow organisiert wurde. In einem Brief an Stassow beschrieb Mussorgskij im Juni 1874 sein neues Projekt:

Ich arbeite mit Volldampf an *Hartmann*, wie ich einst an *Boris* [*Godunov*] mit Volldampf gearbeitet habe; Klänge und Gedanken schwirren nur so in der Luft; ich verschlinge sie und schaffe es kaum, alles aufs Papier zu kritzeln. Ich schreibe an der vierten Nummer – die Übergänge sind geglückt (dank der „Promenaden"). Ich möchte das Ganze möglichst bald und treffend zu Ende bringen. Mein geistiges Abbild erscheint in den Zwischenspielen. Bis jetzt halte ich es für gelungen.[1]

Am 1. Juli schrieb Stassow an Rimskij-Korsakow (1844–1908) über den zweiten Teil des Stückes:

[…] Ich glaube, dass das Beste schon vorhanden ist. „Der Marktplatz von Limoges" ist ein herrliches Scherzino und sehr pianistisch. Dann kommt „Baba-Jaga", das sehr ausdrucksstark ist, und zum Schluss „Das Bogatyr-Tor von Kiew" im Stile eines Chorals oder Finales à la „Slavsia";[2] natürlich [ist es] hundertmillionenmal schlechter und schwächer, aber [es ist] trotzdem ein schönes, ausdrucksvolles, originelles Stück. Hier gibt es einen besonders schönen Choral: „Wie viel euer auf Christum getauft sind", und der Klang der Glocken wird auf eine völlig neue Art und Weise dargestellt. In jenem zweiten Teil gibt es auch ein paar ungewöhnlich poetische Momente. Sie kommen in der Musik zu Hartmanns Bild „Die Kata-

komben von Paris" vor, das aus nichts als Schädeln besteht. Zuerst schildert Musoryanin eine düstere Grotte (mit ausgesprochen orchestral anmutenden Akkorden, die mit einer großen ⌢ lange gehalten werden). Dann folgt über einem Tremolo in Moll das erste Promenadenthema: das Schimmern kleiner Lichter in den Schädeln; hier wird plötzlich Hartmanns magische poetische Anziehungskraft auf Mussorgskij deutlich […]. Doch glauben Sie nicht, Admiral, Musoryanin habe sich nur diesem [Werk] gewidmet: Jetzt ist plötzlich ein solches Verlangen zu komponieren in ihm erwacht, dass für ihn kaum ein Tag ohne vergeht.[3]

Stassows Anmerkungen zum „Klang der Glocken" und den „ausgesprochen orchestral anmutenden Akkorden" erwiesen sich als Prophezeiung: Kein anderes Werk für Klavier wurde so oft für Orchester bearbeitet.

Mussorgskij interpretiert in seinem Klavierzyklus zehn von Hartmanns Werken. Darüber hinaus sind fünf Promenaden eingefügt, in denen die verschiedenen Stimmungen des Komponisten wiedergegeben werden, während er von einem Bild zum nächsten schlendert. Alle Promenaden sind an die Melodie der Eröffnungspromenade angelehnt, die auch in „Mit den Toten in einer toten Sprache" sowie im Finale „Das große Tor von Kiew" vorkommt und somit eine umfassende zyklische Einheit bildet. Die Bilder und ihre musikalische Interpretation können folgendermaßen zusammengefasst werden:

1. „Gnomus" [lat.: Der Zwerg]. In einem Brief an einen Kollegen beschrieb Stassow den geschnitzten Holzzwerg als „eine Art Nussknacker; ein Gnom, in dessen Mund man eine Nuss steckt, um sie zu knacken". Die Musik – grotesk, nervös, jedoch nicht ohne einen Anflug von Tragik – ist ein spiritueller Vorfahre von Ravels „Scarbo" aus *Gaspard de la nuit*.

2. „Il vecchio castello" [ital.: Das alte Schloss]. Hartmanns Bild zeigt ein mittelalterliches italienisches Schloss mit einem singenden

---

[1] Zitiert in Alexandra Orlova, *Mussorgsky's Days and Works*, Übers. und Hrsg. Roy J. Guenther, Ann Arbor 1983, S. 416.

[2] Bezieht sich auf das prunkvolle Finale für Chor und Orchester „Ruhm sei dem Zaren" aus Glinkas Oper *Ein Leben für den Zaren*.

[3] Orlova, a. a. O., S. 419/420.

Troubadour, der sich auf der Laute begleitet. Ein Orgelpunkt auf dem Gis im Bass erstreckt sich über die gesamten 107 Takte dieser bewegenden Serenade.

3. „Tuileries (Dispute d'enfants après jeux)" [frz.: Die Tuilerien (Streit der Kinder nach dem Spiel)]. In seinem Aquarell des berühmten Parks in Paris stellte der Künstler eine Gruppe streitender Kinder in den Mittelpunkt. Mussorgskijs spielerische Interpretation wird nie lauter als *mezzoforte*, und seine Sensibilität für die ursprüngliche Welt der Kinder ist deutlich erkennbar. Eine ähnliche Verschmelzung von Unschuld und Raffinesse ist in Ravels *Ma mère l'oye* und *L'enfant et les sortilèges* zu finden.

4. „Bydło" [polnisch: Ochsenkarren]. Hartmann skizzierte einen Karren mit großen Rädern, der auf einer schlammigen Straße mühsam von zwei Ochsen gezogen wird. Mit ihrem gleichmäßigen, schwerfälligem Rhythmus und slawischen Schwermut erinnert Mussorgskijs Fassung an Chopins Präludium in a-Moll (op. 28 Nr. 2).

5. „Balet nevylupivshikhsa ptentsov" [russisch: Ballett der nicht ausgeschlüpften Küken]. Dies ist der erste von nur drei russischen Titeln in Mussorgskijs Stück. Hartmann malte mehrere Aquarelle als Kostümentwürfe für ein Ballett von Julius Gerber mit dem Titel *Trilby*, das in St. Petersburg aufgeführt wurde. Stassow erklärte, dass die Szene nach einer Gruppe kleiner Jungen und Mädchen verlangte, die wie Kanarienvögel angezogen waren und auf der Bühne herumhüpften. Mussorgskijs flüchtige, zwerghaft anmutende Musik ist in der Form Scherzo, Trio, Scherzo und Coda komponiert.

6. „Samuel Goldenberg und Schmuÿle" [deutsch, eventuell jiddisch: Samuel Goldenberg und Schmuyle]. Der Titel würde im Jiddischen fast genauso klingen, was Mussorgskij eventuell mit dem Trema über dem „y" auszudrücken versuchte. Die Porträts entstanden im polnischen Sandomir und erhielten später von Stassow den Titel „Zwei Juden: der eine reich, der andere arm". Hartmann schenkte Mussorgskij die Porträts als Ausdruck seiner Freundschaft, und der Komponist stellte sie für die Ausstellung seines Kollegen zur Verfügung. In einer kurzen

Äußerung zu seinen ästhetischen Ansichten bemerkte Mussorgskij:

Kunst ist ein Mittel, um mit Menschen zu kommunizieren und kein Selbstzweck […]. Die Mission der Kunst der Musik [ist], nicht nur die Nuancen der Gefühle, sondern, noch wichtiger, die Nuancen der menschlichen Sprache in musikalischen Klängen wiederzugeben.[4]

Der autoritäre Beginn und das demütige Betteln in Mussorgskijs eindrucksvollem Dialog spiegeln seine ästhetische Ansicht hervorragend wider.

7. „Limoges. Le marché (La grande nouvelle)" [frz.: Limoges. Der Marktplatz (Die große Neuigkeit)]. Stassow bestätigte, dass Hartmann ein Bild von einer Menschenmenge auf einem Marktplatz im französischen Limoges gemalt hatte. Das Stimmengewirr und emsige Treiben in diesem Stück (das in Strauss' *Till Eulenspiegels lustige Streiche* wiederkehrt) wurden von Mussorgskij in seinem Manuskript in Worten wiedergegeben, jedoch nachträglich durchgestrichen. Er schrieb auf Französisch:

Die große Neuigkeit: Monsieur Pimpant de Panta-Pantaléon hat gerade seine Kuh namens „Fugitive" wiedergefunden. „Ja, Madame, es war gestern. Nein, Madame, es war vorgestern. Aber ja, Madame, das Tier hat sich in der Nachbarschaft herumgetrieben. Aber nein, Madame, das Tier hat sich überhaupt nicht herumgetrieben." Etc.

8. „Catacombae (Sepulcrum romanum)" [lat.: Die Katakomben (Eine römische Totengruft)]. Dieses düstere Aquarell zeigt Hartmann selbst, einen Kollegen und einen Führer in den Katakomben von Paris. Rechts befinden sich reihenweise menschliche Schädel. Mussorgskijs nicht ganz korrekter lateinischer Titel für den zweiten Teil des Stückes ist in seinem Manuskript mit Bleistift geschrieben: „Con [anstatt „Cum"] mortuis in lingua mortua" [Mit den Toten in einer toten Sprache].[5] Er fügt (auf Russisch) hinzu: „Er kann ruhig auf Lateinisch

---

[4] Malcolm Hamrick Brown (Hrsg.), *Mussorgsky in Memoriam 1881–1981,* Ann Arbor 1982, S. 3.

[5] Obgleich der Titel in Rimskij-Korsakows erster Klavierausgabe der *Bilder einer Ausstellung* korrekt gedruckt ist („Cum"), sind die meisten späteren Ausgaben (sowie Ravels Autograph) falsch („Con").

sein! Der schöpferische Geist des verstorbenen Hartmann führt mich zu den Schädeln und beschwört sie herauf; allmählich beginnen die Schädel zu leuchten." Die beängstigende Finsternis und die Spuren des Übernatürlichen in diesem unheimlichen Diptychon bilden einen starken Gegensatz zu der sorglosen Stimmung des vorherigen Stückes.

9. „Izbushka na kurynikh nozhkakh (Baba-Yaga)" [russisch: Die Hütte auf Hühnerfüßen (Baba-Jaga)]. Hartmanns verschnörkelte Bleistiftzeichnung zeigt eine Uhr im russischen Stil als Teil einer Hexenhütte, die auf Hühnerfüßen steht. Eine hämmernde, stürmische Anfangspassage beschwört den wilden Flug der Hexe Baba-Jaga herauf, die sich von menschlichen Knochen ernährt. Der ruhigere Mittelteil enthält durchgehend geheimnisvoll anmutende Tremolos, und eine Reprise des Anfangsteils führt zu einer Liszt'schen Coda, die das Stück mit dem Finale verbindet. Und so kehren die letzten Bilder nach der Interpretation von Hartmanns künstlerischen Exkursionen nach Italien, Frankreich und Polen zum russischen Volkstum (Baba-Jaga) und zur russischen Geschichte (das Finale) zurück.

10. „Bogatyrskie vorota (vo stolnom gorode vo Kieve)" [russisch: Das Bogatyr-Tor (in der alten Hauptstadt Kiew)]. Hartmanns Entwurf für ein Stadttor wurde für eine Ausschreibung zum Gedenken an ein Ereignis angefertigt, das am 4. April 1866 in Kiew stattfand. Das Ereignis, das von der Zensur verständlicherweise verschwiegen wurde, war das missglückte Attentat auf Zar Alexander II., der es unverletzt überlebte. (Die Ausschreibung wurde abgesagt und das Denkmal nie gebaut.) Hartmann entwarf einen Bogen auf zwei Säulen mit einem Vers aus dem Psalm 118: „Gelobet sei, wer da kommt im Namen des Herrn". Über dem Bogen befand sich eine Kapelle mit Buntglasfenstern, eine Figur des Erzengels Michael und auf dem Dach der russische Reichsadler. Rechts vom Bogen war ein Glockenturm. Das Finale des Komponisten erinnert mit seinen wuchtigen Akkorden, modalen Chorälen und glockenartigen Klängen an eine feierliche Prozession

und gipfelt in einem fulminanten und ausgesprochen orchestralen Schluss.

Der in Russland geborene amerikanische Dirigent Sergej Koussewitzky (1874–1951) beauftragte Ravel mit der Bearbeitung von *Bilder einer Ausstellung*. In einem aufgezeichneten Interview mit dem Verfasser dieses Textes erinnerte sich Ravels Kollege und Biograf Roland-Manuel an deren musikalische Aktivitäten im Sommer 1922.

Ich hatte das Privileg, Ravel bei der Bearbeitung von Mussorgskijs *Bilder einer Ausstellung* zuzusehen. Wir waren im Haus meiner Eltern auf dem Land [in Lyons-la-Fôret, ca. 100 Kilometer nordwestlich von Paris], wo wir uns ein Zimmer teilten, in dem ein Klavier stand. Wir saßen nebeneinander am selben Tisch. Ich arrangierte ein Lied von Debussy, *Le Faune*, während Ravel Mussorgskijs *Bilder einer Ausstellung* für Orchester bearbeitete [...]. Ab und zu zeigte er mir Mussorgskijs Partitur und sagte: „Welches Instrument würdest du hier einsetzen?" „Vielleicht", äußerte ich einmal vorsichtig, „eine Klarinette". „Eine Klarinette?", antwortete er, „Sie ist zu durchdringend!" Also gut, sie ist zu durchdringend. Daraufhin wandte er sich wieder seiner Arbeit zu und sagte später: „Komm, schau." Es war keine Klarinette, sondern ein Saxophon!

Ich sah – was ein großes Privileg war – wie er arrangierte. Es war zwar nicht seine eigene Musik, aber es war trotzdem sehr interessant. Aufmerksam begutachtete er die Passage, an der er arbeitete; er schrieb und verteilte die Instrumente wie jeder andere Arrangeur. Dann, und das kam oft vor, ging er zum Klavier und isolierte eine Instrumentengruppe. Wie er selbst sagte, musste er hören, was eine Gruppe im Verhältnis zu den anderen machte. So sah er sich zum Beispiel an, was die Streicher machten und spielte ihre Stimmen auf dem Klavier. Er sagte, er benutze das Klavier beim Arrangieren viel öfter als beim Komponieren der ersten Fassungen seiner eigenen Werke.[6]

Hinsichtlich Ravels Bedürfnis, Instrumentengruppen zu isolieren, scheint es, dass viele seiner Tutti nach Instrumentenfamilien geordnet sind, wobei jede Instrumentengruppe (natürlich außer den Schlaginstrumenten) Melodie, Har-

---

[6] Das Interview fand am 1. Februar 1966 in der Pariser Wohnung von Roland-Manuel statt.

monien und Basstöne spielt (s. die letzten Takte der Anfangspromenade oder den Schluss von „Das große Tor von Kiew"). Ravels Fähigkeit, unerwartete und einprägsame Orchesterklänge zu erzeugen, wird in seiner Orchesterbearbeitung deutlich: Hier finden sich ausgedehnte Soli für Saxophon („Il vecchio castello") und Tuba („Bydło"). In „Gnomus" (Ziffer 9) wiederholt Mussorgskij die vorangegangenen zehn Takte, doch Ravel instrumentiert die Passage um – diesmal mit Celesta (als Ersatz für die Holzbläser), begleitet von Streicherglissandi auf dem Griffbrett. Schmuyles Betteln wird (auf etwas paradoxe Weise) durch eine gedämpfte Trompete vermittelt, die *fortissimo* spielt (Ziffer 58). Neben den vielen Feinheiten bei den Schlaginstrumenten (z. B. bei Ziffer 55 oder ab Ziffer 121) kommt eine von Ravels auffälligsten Passagen für Blechbläser (begleitet von Holzbläsern und Kontrabässen) in den „Katakomben" vor. Im Allgemeinen weist die Bearbeitung auf eine starke Angleichung an Rimskij-Korsakows Bearbeitungstechnik hin, verbunden mit Ravels Vorliebe für einen Klang, der, wie er es ausdrückte, „von einer volltönenden Flüssigkeit umflutet" ist.[7]

Obwohl *Bilder einer Ausstellung* zweifellos Mussorgskijs bedeutendstes Klavierwerk ist, wurde es von Pianisten in Russland und anderen Ländern jahrelang vernachlässigt. Merkwürdigerweise wurde das Stück erst dann auch von Pianisten gespielt, nachdem Ravels Bearbeitung weltweite Anerkennung erlangt hatte. Professor Malcolm H. Brown bezeichnete Ravels Leistung als „ein seltenes Beispiel für eine kreative Symbiose, die erst durch Bewunderer beider Komponisten zur Geltung kommt"[8], und Arturo Toscanini erklärte, dass „die beiden großen Abhandlungen über Instrumentierung die von Berlioz sowie Ravels Orchesterfassung der *Bilder einer Ausstellung* waren."[9]

Letztendlich ist Ravels Orchesterfassung eine brillante Hommage an Mussorgskij, dessen Musik er viele Jahre lang studierte und zutiefst bewunderte.

Arbie Orenstein
Übersetzung: Heike Brühl

---

[7] Vgl. Arbie Orenstein, *Ravel: Man and Musicians*, New York 1991, S.126. Ravel bemerkte einmal, dass man in der Kunst der Orchesterbearbeitung immer noch etwas dazulernen könne. Er bearbeitete nicht nur viele seiner eigenen Klavierwerke, sondern auch Werke von Chabrier, Chopin, Debussy, Schumann, Satie und anderen.
[8] Brown, a. a. O., S. 6.
[9] Harvey Sachs, *Toscanini*, London 1978, S. 316.

Textual Notes

AUT = Ravel's orchestral autograph
IE = First orchestral edition
KOUS = Serge Koussevitzky
MUSS = Mussorgsky's piano holograph
R-K = Rimsky-Korsakov's piano edition
WU = Wiener Urtext piano edition
Br. = Brass
Str. = Strings
Ww. = Woodwind
Orch. = Orchestra
b(b) = bar(s)
n(n) = note(s)
l.h. = left hand
r.h. = right hand

Promenade (p. 1)

Tbn. 3 as IE but in AUT this for Tbn. 2

bar 23 Pfte. n1 e♭ as MUSS, R-K; Orch. e♮ (Cor. 3 b♮) as AUT, IE, apparently Ravel's emendation

1. Gnomus (p. 6)

10, 17 Ptti. stacc. dot in AUT, not IE. Str. wedges in AUT; IE stacc. dots.

40 Arpa as IE; AUT

Pfte. 34 R-K n2 B♭ octaves followed in Orch. b44 by AUT, IE Cl. b (c′) Fg., Cfg., Vc., Cb.

68 Cor., Tr, Str. AUT (Ravel) 'le ré est bon (cors et trompettes id.)' ['D is correct – the same for the horns and trumpets']; KOUS writes 'Mi♭ (Moussorgsky)'; MUSS, R-K E♭, which is played in KOUS recording (see fn. 14). Tr. 1 AUT, IE n5 ♭ lacking.

70 G.C. *f* as AUT; IE *mf*. Dynamics throughout frequently standardized in IE, whereas AUT appears more carefully worked out.

82 Cor. 2 AUT 'hauteur réelle' [actual pitch], i.e. to sound a perfect 5th below written note. Ravel consistently adds this phrase when Cor. are notated in bass clef to avoid the older custom of playing bass clef notation up a perfect 4th.

83ff. Vc. *gliss.* in IE, not AUT

100 Cb. AUT, IE lacking ♭

Promenade (p. 20)

Orch. tempo by analogy with Pfte.

10 Pfte. R-K beats 4, 5 D♭ followed in AUT, IE Fl. 2/3, Fg. 1/2

2. Il vecchio castello (p. 21)

3ff. Fg. 1 nn4–5 ♩♩♩ as IE; AUT ♩♩♩

15 C. ing. crotchet as MUSS; R-K quaver

19   AUT additional bar; not MUSS, R-K

32/33,   Cb. as AUT; IE
41/42

62–69   Fg. 2 IE

63, 64,   Cb. IE lacking arco
82, 83

    99   Pfte. R-K *l.h.* n2 b tied to n1, followed in AUT, IE; MUSS a♯

Promenade (p. 33)

    MUSS, R-K, AUT, WU 'Moderato non tanto, pesamente [*sic*]', IE 'Moderato non tanto, pesante'; Mussorgsky probably intended 'pesantemente'. Cl. 1/2, Cl. b. AUT, IE key signature 3 sharps

3. Tuileries (p. 35)

   8, 9   Pfte. R-K *r.h.* n7 g♮″ followed in AUT, IE Fl. 1/2, Cl. 1/2 (b♭″)

    17   Pfte. R-K *l.h.* n4 f♯′ followed in AUT, IE Vl. II

    29   Pfte. R-K *r.h.* n1 a♯′ not b′, AUT Cl. 1 d″ in ink later changed in pencil to c♯″ following R-K; IE c♯″

4. Bydło (p. 41)

    1   Pfte. R-K *pp poco a poco cresc.* followed in AUT, IE

    8   Pfte. R-K *l.h.* n4 D♯ not C♯ followed in AUT, IE Fg. 2

   21   Vc. AUT n3 (lower) D♮ corrected to D♯ by KOUS

   24   Pfte. R-K n1 *r.h.* crotchet followed in AUT, IE

   37   Arpa AUT, IE *r.h.*

   43   Str. AUT *dim.* begins b42

5. Ballet des poussins dans leurs coques (p. 52)

   5ff.   Ww. IE incorrectly shows grace doubled by Ob. 2, Fl. 2, Cl. 2

 20, 74   Cl. 2 AUT, IE n1 lacking ♭

 31–37   Fl. 1/2 beat 1 as IE; AUT

 31–38   Vla. AUT, IE a, apparently an oversight

   36   Fl. 1, Cel. AUT grace note originally without ♯, added by Ravel later (c♯‴ in R-K) – queried by KOUS

 47–74   Written out in full in IE; AUT not written out, instead at the end of the Trio Ravel (and MUSS, R-K, WU) has 'Da capo il scherzino senza trio, e poi coda'. At the end of the scherzino, however, bb21, 22 are within an ending bracket over the system, unlike MUSS, R-K, WU, thus shortening Mussorgsky's reprise by two bars. Over the system bb75–78 AUT has a mirror image of the bracket at bb21, 22.

   74   Vl. I n4, b75 n1 as IE; these notes not in AUT (cf. bb19, 20)

   75   Pfte. see bb47–74 above

6. Samuel Goldenberg und Schmuÿle (p. 62)

    1   Orch. nn6–10 AUT, IE rhythm follows R-K misreading of MUSS.

19 Tr. 1/2 n16, b21 n6, b23 n11 ✕ as AUT, IE (G♭ in MUSS, R-K). (KOUS places a sharp sign over each of these notes in AUT and plays f♯″/f♯′ in his recording.)

23 Cl. b. n5 c♯′ as AUT, lacking in IE; Fg. 1/2 IE n5

26, 27 Ob. 1, Cl. b., Vl. I/II, Vla., Vc. IE last 2 notes

28 Pfte. R-K n8 C (double octaves) followed in AUT, IE

7. Limoges (p. 72)

5, 30 Tri. IE *f*

6 Cor. 1/3 nn6–9, b7 n1 as IE, lacking in AUT but cf. bb31, 32

10 Cor. 1/3 AUT, IE n1 slur missing, oversight apparently due to page turn in AUT (cf. bb27, 28 which appear correctly in AUT, IE)

11 Cl. 1/2 IE n6 f″/d″

16, 17 Vl. II, Vla. dynamics as AUT; IE b17 dynamics as b16

18, 19 Tr. 1 as IE; AUT

22 Vl. I AUT, IE n2♭ not ♮

24 Arpa as IE; AUT rhythm

25 Camp. *ff* as IE, lacking in AUT

27, 34 Pfte. R-K *l.h.* nn1–4 g′/e♭′ followed in AUT, IE b27 Tr. 2, Vl. II, Vla., b34 Cor. 1/2, Vla., Vc.

36 Ptti. ——— in IE not AUT; Arpa ——— by analogy. Orch. *f* in IE not AUT.

37 C. ing. IE > moved to n2

40 Ob. 1/2 AUT last 2 notes tied; Tr. IE n9 a 2; Vla. nn1–15 as IE, in AUT; Vc. AUT, IE n8 (cf. Vl. I/II, Vla. final note). Pfte. WU *l.h.* n13 ♮ lacking; WU *l.h.* no correcting accidentals offered for same pitches inflected in *r.h.* throughout bar.

8. Catacombae (p. 85)

5–6 Cor. 3/4 slur in IE, not AUT

6, 7 Tbn. 1–3, Tuba |*ff* |*p* | by analogy bb4, 5; R-K bb4/5, 6/7 |*ffsf* |*p dim.* |

12 Pfte. R-K *l.h.* adds BB, followed in AUT, IE Cfg.

20–21 Pfte. *l.h.* AA–AA tie across barline as MUSS, lacking in WU

28–29 Fg. 1 IE slur across barline

30 Tam-t. AUT fermata on beat 3 rest, IE fermata on minim and beat 3 rest

(Cum mortuis in lingua mortua)

31 tempo from MUSS, WU

31–33 Vl. I as IE; AUT

Ravel inadvertently added stems to semibreve noteheads in bb32, 33 but may have intended dotted minim at b31 following R-K (MUSS).

37 Cl. 1 n3 e′ (= c♯″) as AUT, IE; MUSS, R-K c♮″, WU editorial c♯″

42–45 Ob. KOUS in AUT '1 ob. solo', IE Ob. 1/2

46–51 Arpa IE key sig. 2 ♯'s

51 Fl. 1/2 harmonics in IE, not AUT; Vla. *trem.* in IE, not AUT

9. La cabane sur des pattes de poule (Baba-Yaga) (p. 92)

10–16 Cor. 1–4 stacc. dots in IE, not AUT

30 (144) Cl. 1 AUT, IE beat 2 lacking ♮

53, 54 Cor. 1–4 ⸺ from KOUS in AUT
(167, 168)

58 (180) Cl. 1/2 AUT, IE n3 ♮ lacking

73 Tbn. 3, Tuba n1 ∧ by analogy (cf. b187 ∧ in IE), not in AUT

74 Pfte. R-K *r.h.*  on which AUT Str. *gliss.* are based

95, 96 Orch. (Tr. 1) Ravel (AUT, IE) adds two bars, neither in MUSS, R-K

98ff. Fg. 1 pencilled in AUT, originally scored for Sax. a. in ink and crossed
out. KOUS wrote 'Sax.' (as a cue) suggesting that Ravel's change was a
late one. Ravel notated 'sourdines' for Cb. but crossed it out.

106 Vc., Cb. as Ravel's correction in AUT, not IE. Ravel wrote in pencil that
the note A and the indications sourdines and pizz. should be removed and
replaced by a minim rest, and that the *p* comes later on the third beat.

106, 107 Vl. I div. in unison on 2 staves in AUT (Vl. II tacet); IE designates Vl. I
(2) as Vl. II

107 Cl. b. n1 *mf* in IE, *p* in AUT

111 Vl. II AUT *trem.* 𝄥 , b112 𝄥 ; standardized in IE, present edition when-
ever inconsistent to 𝄥

118 Vla. con sord. as IE, lacking in AUT; ditto Vc. b119, Cb. b123

119 Cfg. *f* as IE. Vl. II as AUT; IE ♪ 𝄾

123 Xilo. as IE, lacking in AUT apparently due to a page turn

125 Vc., Cb. senza sord. in IE, lacking in AUT

127–134 Tuba, Timp. as AUT; IE

138 KOUS in AUT writes: 'reprendre de [figs.] 82 = 95 à 102 puis coda 102'
[repeat from figs. 82(=95)–102 and then the coda at 102]. Beginning at
b25 (fig. 82), the following figs. and their equivalents are noted by
Ravel: 82=95, 83=96, 84=97, 85=98, 86=99, 87=100, 88=101, 89=102.
At fig. 89 Ravel writes 'al coda'. Thus the music from figs. 95–102 is
not written out, being the same as figs. 82–89.

199–202 Fg. 1/2 4-bar slur as AUT; IE two 2-bar slurs

213 Vl. I/II, Vc. AUT, IE n4 𝅘𝅥 ; Vla. nn1–4 AUT ♩♩♩♩ , IE ♬♬

10. La grande porte de Kiev (p. 121)

1 Pfte. time sig. 𝄴 in MUSS, R-K, followed in AUT; WU 𝄵

6 Pfte. R-K *l.h.* n1 [musical notation] probably engraver's error

8 Pfte. R-K *l.h.* n1 G not F, followed (also b6) in AUT, 1E Fg. 2, Cor. 4 (d′)

17 Pfte. R-K *l.h.* n2 no e♭, followed in AUT, 1E with no equivalent e♭

30 Pfte. R-K *r.h.* a♭′ not e♭′, followed in AUT, 1E Cl. 1 b♭′ (=a♭′)

60 Pfte. R-K *r.h.* n1 f″ not e♭″, not followed in AUT, 1E

64 Pfte. R-K *p*, followed in AUT, 1E

85–88 Vl. II, Vla. (upper), Vc. (upper) phrased as AUT; 1E [musical notation]

93 KOUS in AUT writes 'accelerando cresc.'

102, 103 Fl. 1/2, Ob. 1–3, Cl. 1/2 as 1E (Fl. n1 editor's parentheses);

AUT (see Preface)

b102 Vl. I (upper), Vl. II (upper), Vla. (upper) *trem.* [musical notation] as 1E; AUT [musical notation]

105, 106 Cor. 3 AUT, 1E b♭–b♭, probably an oversight for Cor. 4

111–114 Orch. as 1E; AUT doubles bb111–113 and note values, adds two extra bars not in R-K (MUSS) which in 1E become halved (b114). See Preface.

115, 119 Timp. B♭ as AUT; 1E e♭

123, 124 Fl. 3 AUT, where Fl. 1, 2 share a staff, Ravel apparently forgot to write 'col I°', hence 1E follows similarly

146 Pfte. R-K *r.h.* [musical notation] , probably engraver's error unwittingly taken into AUT; present edition brings Orch. notation into conformance with MUSS

146–147 Cor. 2 tie by analogy with Cor. 3

163 'Les petites notes sur le temps' in AUT, not 1E; Vc., Cb. down-bow added by analogy with other Str.

167 Vl. II (lower) grace note changed editorially; AUT, 1E have improbable

[musical notation]

169 Pfte. R-K omits grace notes, followed in AUT, 1E

179–182 Str. [musical notation] added by KOUS in AUT, taken into 1E; Ww. Br., Perc. [musical notation] by analogy

Arbie Orenstein

TABLEAUX D'UNE EXPOSITION

Modest Petrovich Mussorgsky
(1839–1881)
Orchestrated by/Orchestriert von
Maurice Ravel
(1875–1937)

Promenade

Edited by Arbie Orenstein
© 2016 Ernst Eulenburg Ltd, London
and Ernst Eulenburg & Co GmbH, Mainz

attacca

1. Gnomus
The Gnome
Der Zwerg

10

12

14

15

20

Promenade

attacca

2. Il vecchio castello
The Old Castle
Das alte Schloss

Promenade

34

attacca

3. Tuileries
(Dispute d'enfants après jeux)
(Children Quarrelling After Play)
(Streit der Kinder nach dem Spiel)

4. Bydło
[Le bétail]
[Cattle]
[Das Vieh]

★ Otez les sourdines une à une jusqu'à 39

42

48

★ Mettez progressivement les sourdines jusqu'à 45

Promenade

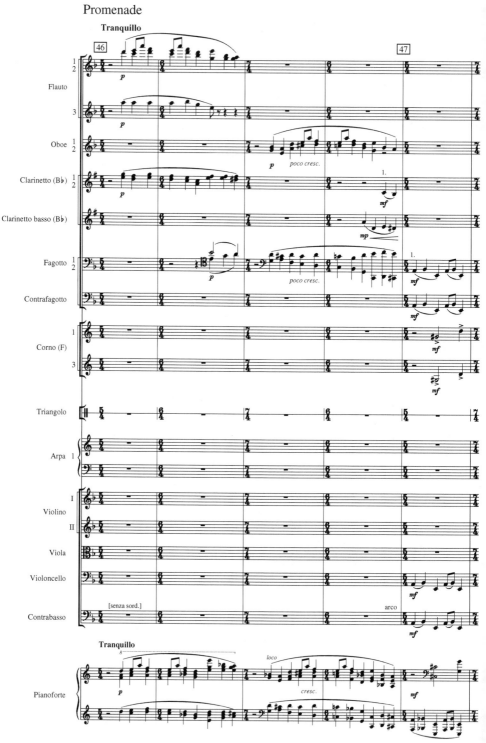

5. Ballet des poussins dans leurs coques
Ballet of the Unhatched Chicks
Ballett der nicht ausgeschlüpften Küken

Trio

60

Coda

attacca

6. Samuel Goldenberg und Schmuÿle

7. Limoges
   Le marché (La grande nouvelle)
   The Market Place (Important News)
   Der Marktplatz (Die große Neuigkeit)

80

8. Catacombae (Sepulcrum romanum)
   Catacombs (A Roman Sepulchre)
   Die Katakomben (Eine römische Totengruft)

Cum mortuis in lingua mortua
With the Dead in a Dead Language
Mit den Toten in einer toten Sprache

9. La cabane sur des pattes de poule (Baba-Yaga)
   The Hut on Hen's Legs (Baba-Yaga)
   Die Hütte auf Hühnerfüßen (Baba-Jaga)

120

attacca

10. La grande porte de Kiev
The Great Gate of Kiev
Das große Tor von Kiew

122

134

138

120 **Poco a poco rallentando**

144

★ Les petites notes sur le temps

146